SAFE BY DESIGN
SAFE
TRANSPORTATION

by Kaitlyn Duling

po go

Ideas for Parents and Teachers

Pogo Books let children practice reading informational text while introducing them to nonfiction features such as headings, labels, sidebars, maps, and diagrams, as well as a table of contents, glossary, and index.

Carefully leveled text with a strong photo match offers early fluent readers the support they need to succeed.

Before Reading

- "Walk" through the book and point out the various nonfiction features. Ask the student what purpose each feature serves.
- Look at the glossary together. Read and discuss the words.

Read the Book

- Have the child read the book independently.
- Invite him or her to list questions that arise from reading.

After Reading

- Discuss the child's questions. Talk about how he or she might find answers to those questions.
- Prompt the child to think more. Ask: What modes of transportation do you take each day? How do you stay safe while you use them?

Pogo Books are published by Jump!
5357 Penn Avenue South
Minneapolis, MN 55419
www.jumplibrary.com

Library of Congress Cataloging-in-Publication Data
is available at www.loc.gov or upon request from
the publisher.

ISBN: 978-1-64128-881-1 (hardcover)
ISBN: 978-1-64128-882-8 (paperback)
ISBN: 978-1-64128-883-5 (ebook)

Editor: Susanne Bushman
Designer: Michelle Sonnek

Photo Credits: MCCAIG/iStock, cover; Brent Hofacker/
Shutterstock, 1 (left), 1 (middle); Hank Shiffman/
Shutterstock, 1 (right); Kaesler Media/Shutterstock, 3;
Pepperer85/Shutterstock, 4; StonePhotos/Shutterstock,
5; Makhh/Shutterstock, 6-7; fStop/Getty, 8-9, 14;
Mike Kuhlman/Shutterstock, 10; Sundry Photography/
Shutterstock, 11; PanicAttack/Shutterstock,
12-13; barbsimages/Shutterstock, 15; Denis Tabler/
Shutterstock, 16-17; MsSponge/iStock, 18-19; dpa
picture alliance archive/Alamy, 20-21; Odua Images/
Shutterstock, 23.

Printed in the United States of America at
Corporate Graphics in North Mankato, Minnesota.

TABLE OF CONTENTS

CHAPTER 1

SAFETY FIRST

Screech! What's that sound? It is an **automatic train stop**. It stops a train if there is a problem. It is just one of many ways to keep travelers safe!

Everyone must travel safely. There can be many **modes** of transportation at an **intersection**. Cars wait at a traffic light. Bikes wait, too. People walk in crosswalks.

Transportation engineers help keep us moving. How? They plan systems like highways, subways, and crosswalks. Designers help, too. They create technology, like backup cameras. These help us avoid accidents.

DID YOU KNOW?

The United States has more than four million miles (6.4 million kilometers) of roads. There are 200,000 miles (321,869 km) of railway. There are more than 5,000 public airports!

highways

Transportation engineers create **models** and perform tests. Why? They use them to test out systems and technologies. **Data** from the tests helps them solve problems.

CHAPTER 2

· ·

RULES OF THE ROAD

Driving too fast can be dangerous. Transportation engineers created speed limits and speed bumps. These help manage drivers' speed.

speed bump · · · · ▶

Traffic lights help control city traffic. Transportation engineers decide how long each one lasts. They want traffic to flow smoothly.

traffic light

Market St

NO U TURN

Road signs tell us how to stay safe. Stop signs are red octagons. Warning signs are yellow diamonds. They tell us to watch out! They can warn us of turns, animals, and more. Speed limits are white squares. They tell drivers how fast to drive.

TAKE A LOOK!

What do these common road signs mean?

Bike Lane
alerts drivers to share the road with cyclists

Pedestrian Crossing
warns drivers about possible pedestrians in the street

Railroad Crossing
alerts drivers to be aware of trains

Slippery When Wet
warns drivers that road may be slippery during rain or snow

CHAPTER 3

· ·

SAFE ON THE GO

Features in cars keep us safe, too. Passive features protect us during accidents. **Airbags** do this. They fill with air if there is a crash. They cushion your body.

airbag · · · · ▶

0001768

Active features help prevent accidents. **Lane-support systems** are one. They let the driver know if the car crosses into another lane. New features can tell when a driver is sleepy. Alarms sound to wake the driver up!

lane

Many cars have cameras and **sensors**. They help keep drivers in their lanes. **Hands-free systems** help, too. They let drivers use phones with only their voices! The driver is less distracted. Hands stay on the steering wheel.

hands-free system

Calling Home...

TAKE A LOOK!

Cars are full of safety features. Take a look!

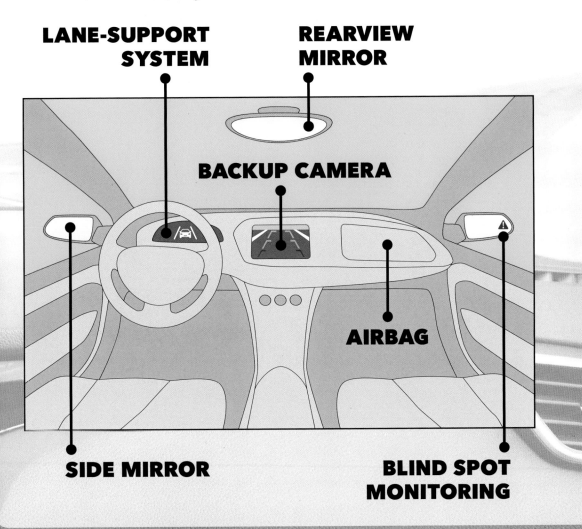

LANE-SUPPORT SYSTEM

REARVIEW MIRROR

BACKUP CAMERA

AIRBAG

SIDE MIRROR

BLIND SPOT MONITORING

Click! Fasten your seat belt. Seat belts keep us secure. They save more than 15,000 lives each year. Some **inflate** during a crash. Why? They cushion the head and neck.

DID YOU KNOW?

Seat belts were invented in the 1950s. They were not required in cars until 1966!

Streets and roads are busy. The air is less busy. But airplanes still need safety features! Like what? Airplanes have exit windows and safety slides in case of a crash. There are life vests for water landings.

What if you were a transportation engineer? How would you keep people moving safely?

DID YOU KNOW?

Airplanes are one of the safest forms of travel. Bad accidents only happen in about one out of every two million flights!

safety slide

ACTIVITIES & TOOLS

MAKE YOUR OWN CITY

Design your own town! What do you need to include to make it safe?

What You Need:

- a roll of paper or extra-large poster board
- crayons or colored pencils
- cardboard boxes or cereal boxes
- tape
- scissors
- toy cars, airplanes, and trains

① **First, sketch out your town. What shape will it be? What types of buildings and houses will it have?**

② **Use the boxes and tape to make some buildings for your city.**

③ **Think about the cars, trains, and airplanes you have. Will you need to build an airport or train station? How will people get to those stations?**

④ **Consider what your city will look like during rush hour when many people are traveling. You may need to add more streets, stoplights, buses, or roundabouts.**

⑤ **When you have finished your city, try other designs. Think about special problems you can solve, like building a city in the mountains or creating a town that doesn't use any electricity.**

GLOSSARY

airbags: Bags in cars that automatically inflate during an accident to protect passengers.

automatic train stop: A system that can stop a train to prevent accidents.

data: Information that can be used for planning.

hands-free systems: Technologies that allow drivers to operate their cell phones without their hands.

inflate: To expand by filling with air.

intersection: A place where two or more roads meet.

lane-support systems: Technologies in cars that help drivers stay in their lanes.

models: Representations of real situations, systems, or events.

modes: Particular types or varieties of something.

sensors: Instruments that can detect and measure changes and transmit the information to a controlling device.

transportation engineers: People who design, analyze, and manage systems and facilities related to transportation.

INDEX

TO LEARN MORE

Finding more information is as easy as 1, 2, 3.

1 Go to www.factsurfer.com

2 Enter "safetransportation" into the search box.

3 Choose your book to see a list of websites.

FACT SURFER